EDGE BOOKS™

VAMPIRES

Great Vampire Legends

by Mandy R. Marx

Consultant: Elizabeth Miller
Professor Emeritus
Memorial University of Newfoundland

CAPSTONE PRESS
a capstone imprint

Edge Books are published by Capstone Press,
151 Good Counsel Drive, P.O. Box 669, Mankato, Minnesota 56002.
www.capstonepub.com

 Books published by Capstone Press are manufactured with paper
containing at least 10 percent post-consumer waste.

Library of Congress Cataloging-in-Publication Data
Marx, Mandy R.
  Great vampire legends / by Mandy R. Marx.
    p. cm.—(Edge books. Vampires)
  Includes bibliographical references and index.
  Summary: "Presents vampire legends throughout history"—Provided
by publisher.
  ISBN 978-1-4296-4576-8 (library binding)
  1. Vampires—Juvenile literature. I. Title. II. Series.
  BF1556.M345 2011
  398'.45—dc22   2010001689

Editorial Credits
Megan Peterson, editor; Veronica Correia, designer; Marcie Spence,
    media researcher; Laura Manthe, production specialist

Photo Credits
Alamy/Photos 12, 28
Art Resource, N.Y./V&A Images, London, 21
Collection Kharbine-Tapabor, Paris, France/The Bridgeman Art Library
    International, 12–13
Fortean Picture Library, 25
Getty Images Inc./DEA/G. Dagli Orti, 17; Hungarian School, 15
The Granger Collection, New York, 19, 27
iStockphoto/grapix, 5
Jeff L. Davis, 22
Mary Evans Picture Library, 7, 18
Newscom, 29
Ryan P. Hutcherson, 23
ullstein bild/The Granger Collection, New York, cover
Wikimedia/Jappalang, 9; Wernain S., 11

The author dedicates this book to Grace, her own little vampire
    with a heart of gold.

TABLE OF
CONTENTS

Chapter 1

Vampire on the Prowl

In an eastern European village in the late 1600s, something strange is happening. First an old man grows weak and ill. Within days, he dies.

Soon after his burial, his family members also get sick. One by one, they die. The frightened townspeople suspect vampire activity. It is a common belief that vampires target their family members.

The townsfolk dig up the body of the first man to die. Sure enough, he shows all the signs of being a vampire. His hair and nails have grown. His skin has not rotted. His body is **bloated**. No doubt it is full of other people's blood. And there is a trickle of blood dripping out of his mouth.

bloated—swollen with fluid or gas

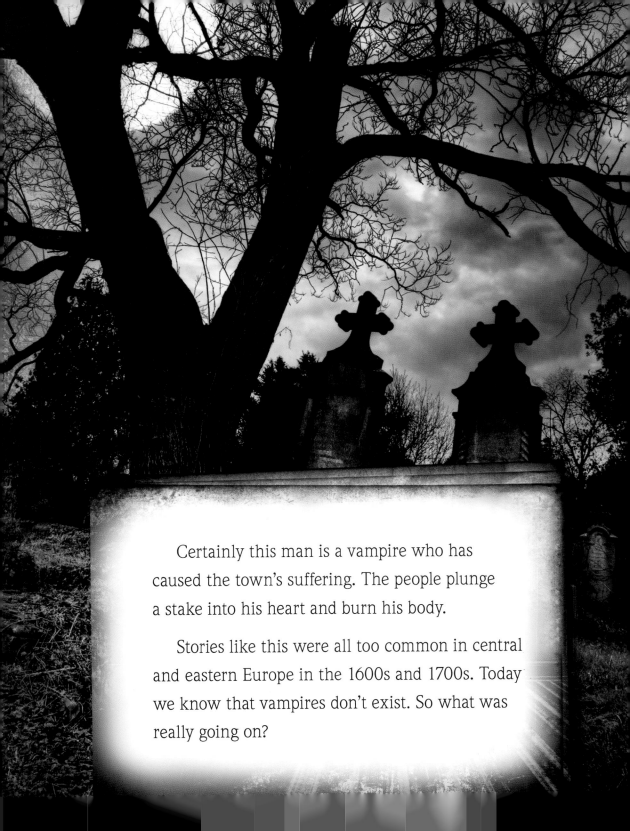

Certainly this man is a vampire who has caused the town's suffering. The people plunge a stake into his heart and burn his body.

Stories like this were all too common in central and eastern Europe in the 1600s and 1700s. Today we know that vampires don't exist. So what was really going on?

Creatures of the Night

Bloodthirsty vampires hide in the shadows of our imagination. But for thousands of years, people believed they were real creatures. Almost every **culture** had its own idea of a vampire. Some vampires had hooves or hooks instead of feet. Most vampires were thought to drink blood. Others stole food or sucked power from animals. If a vampire took power from a cow, that cow could no longer give milk.

Why did so many cultures have vampire legends? Ancient people may have developed a belief in vampires to help understand the world around them. They often blamed vampires for unexplained illnesses and deaths. If cows stopped giving milk, vampire attacks seemed to be the only explanation that made sense. The belief in vampires hung around until scientists proved they couldn't be real.

culture—a people's way of life, ideas, customs, and traditions

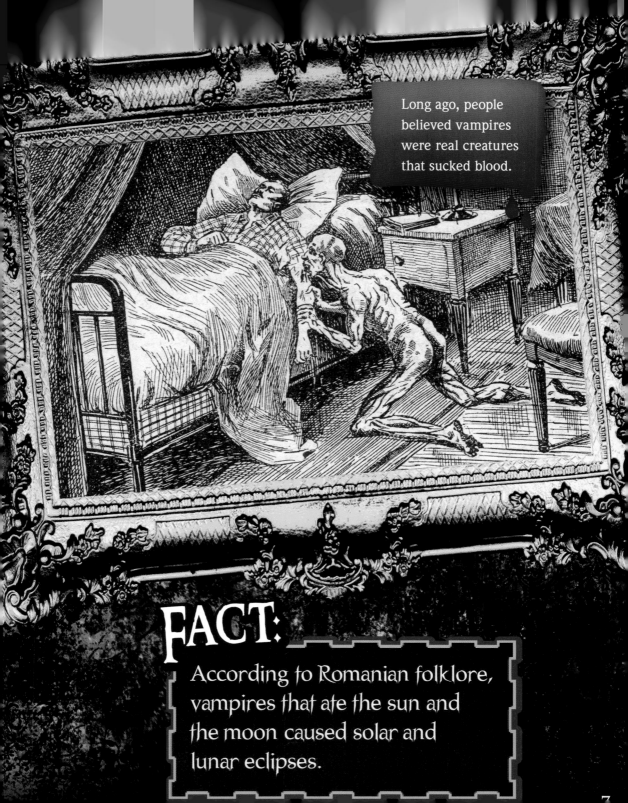

Long ago, people believed vampires were real creatures that sucked blood.

FACT:

According to Romanian folklore, vampires that ate the sun and the moon caused solar and lunar eclipses.

Chapter 2

THE EARLIEST LEGENDS

The popular myth of the modern-day vampire began in central and eastern Europe about 500 years ago. Unlike today's good-looking vampires, these first vampires were disgusting. People imagined they were terrifying corpses that hunted the living. Stories were handed down of dead bodies rising from their graves to attack loved ones. These stories seemed to be proven by actual events and recorded experiences.

A Stranger's Visit

One vampire legend tells of a Hungarian soldier who stayed with a family in 1715. The family and the solider sat down to eat a meal. Soon a strange man appeared in the doorway. The man's visit upset the family members. But they allowed him to join them for supper. The confused soldier didn't know what to think.

Stories of vampires leaving their graves to attack humans were common in central and eastern Europe.

The next morning, the man of the house was found dead. The stranger was the man's father who had been dead for 10 years. The family believed he was a vampire who had claimed his son's life.

Arnold Paole

In 1727, Serbian soldier Arnold Paole died when a hay cart fell on him. Soon after his death, people began to have visions of him. They believed Paole had become a vampire.

Paole himself had once complained of being attacked by a vampire. He was afraid that he would also become a vampire after death. To "cure" himself, Paole ate soil from the vampire's grave. He even rubbed the vampire's blood on himself. Apparently these measures didn't work. Four people in Paole's village died mysteriously a month after his death.

A Vampire Scholar

In the early 1700s, a monk named Augustin Calmet traveled across Europe. He interviewed people about suspected vampire sightings. Calmet included the stories of the Hungarian soldier and Arnold Paole in his book The Phantom World.

Statue of Augustin Calmet

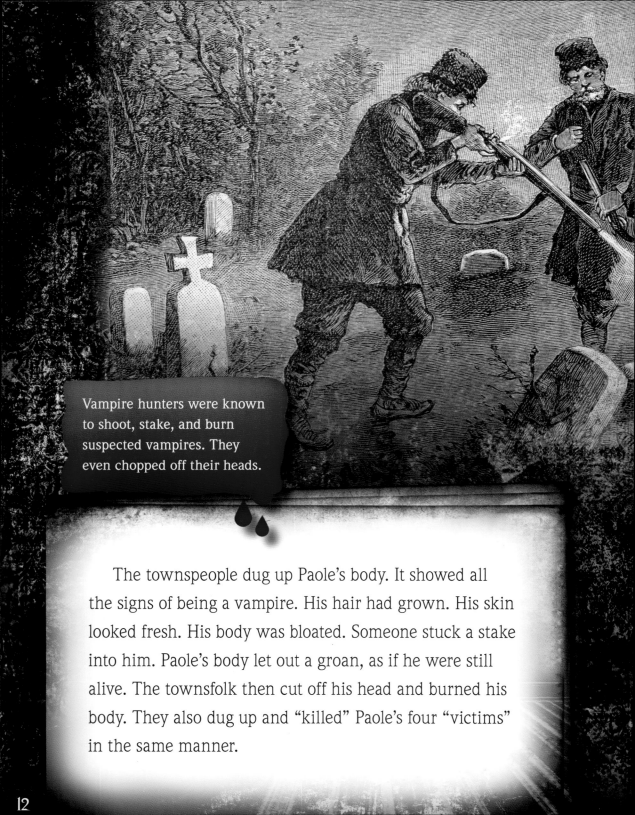

Vampire hunters were known to shoot, stake, and burn suspected vampires. They even chopped off their heads.

The townspeople dug up Paole's body. It showed all the signs of being a vampire. His hair had grown. His skin looked fresh. His body was bloated. Someone stuck a stake into him. Paole's body let out a groan, as if he were still alive. The townsfolk then cut off his head and burned his body. They also dug up and "killed" Paole's four "victims" in the same manner.

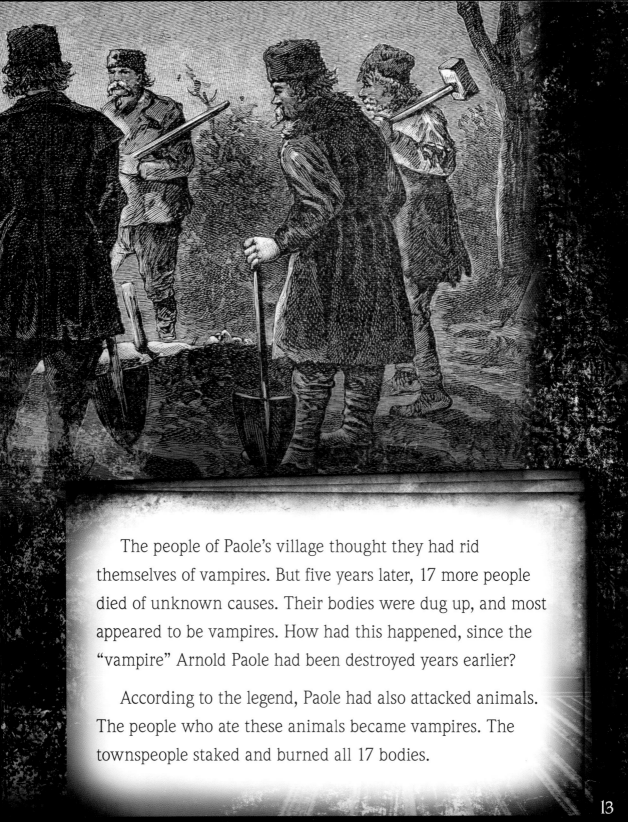

The people of Paole's village thought they had rid themselves of vampires. But five years later, 17 more people died of unknown causes. Their bodies were dug up, and most appeared to be vampires. How had this happened, since the "vampire" Arnold Paole had been destroyed years earlier?

According to the legend, Paole had also attacked animals. The people who ate these animals became vampires. The townspeople staked and burned all 17 bodies.

Vampires in America

The vampire myth eventually made its way to America. In 1896, the *New York World* printed a story about vampires in Rhode Island. Some Rhode Islanders believed **tuberculosis** turned people into vampires. Most cases were reported in families in which many people died of the disease. The surviving family members believed their dead loved ones had become vampires. The vampires then spread the disease to their family members. The survivors dug up the bodies and burned the corpses' hearts. They believed this was the only way to avoid vampire attacks.

FACT:

In Europe, people sometimes removed the hearts of suspected vampires' corpses.

tuberculosis—a disease caused by bacteria that causes fever, weight loss, coughing, and sometimes death

The Blood Countess

Elisabeth Bathory was a Hungarian royal who lived in the late 1500s and early 1600s. She beat, burned, and cut her servant girls. Bathory squeezed some girls into small, spike-filled cages. Most of the girls were beaten to death. It is believed that Bathory killed more than 600 girls. Stories tell of her bathing in her victims' blood. Bathory may have believed that bathing in young girls' blood would stop her from aging.

Eventually Bathory was caught and punished for her crimes. She spent the remaining years of her life locked inside a room in her castle.

Chapter 3

The Truth about Vampires

Today we know that there is no such thing as a vampire. So what really happened to cause a widespread belief in vampires? We can't know for sure, but experts do have some explanations.

One idea is that some people were accidentally buried alive. If they dug out of their graves, they might have been mistaken for vampires.

A more reasonable explanation is that people used vampires to explain outbreaks of deadly diseases. Hundreds of years ago, people had no knowledge of **contagious** diseases. Entire families sometimes died during **plagues**. People often thought the first family member to die was a vampire.

contagious—easily spread
plague—a serious disease that spreads quickly to many people
          and often causes death

During plagues, vampires were sometimes blamed for spreading disease.

The Science Behind Vampirism

What causes vampire "symptoms" if vampires don't exist? Let's tackle these symptoms one at a time.

People sometimes claimed to have visions of vampires. These people may have been sick with high fevers. The fevers could have caused **hallucinations**.

High fevers may have fueled the belief in vampires.

The growth of a corpse's hair and nails after death must have been shocking. But that is not what really happened. When a person dies, their body loses moisture. This causes the skin to shrink and tighten. The tightened skin makes the hair and nails look longer.

The skin of a vampire was also said to still look fresh. Why hadn't the person's body decayed? If a person is poisoned, their body tissues might take longer to break down. Cooler underground temperatures can also cause body tissues to decay more slowly.

hallucination—something seen that is not really there
microorganism—a living thing too small to be seen without a microscope

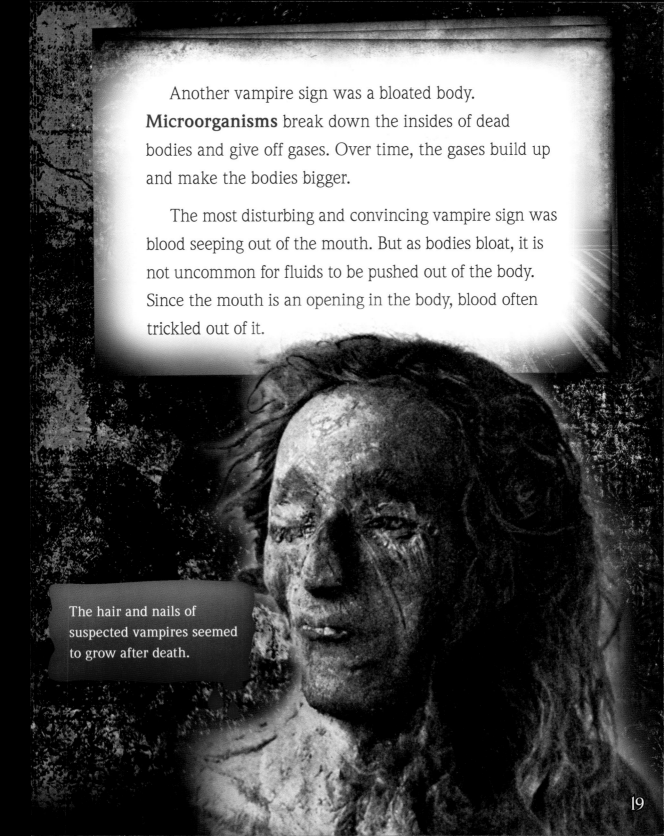

Another vampire sign was a bloated body. **Microorganisms** break down the insides of dead bodies and give off gases. Over time, the gases build up and make the bodies bigger.

The most disturbing and convincing vampire sign was blood seeping out of the mouth. But as bodies bloat, it is not uncommon for fluids to be pushed out of the body. Since the mouth is an opening in the body, blood often trickled out of it.

The hair and nails of suspected vampires seemed to grow after death.

19

Chapter 4

Vampires
Around the World

The most popular image of the vampire is based on European legends. But bloodsucking monsters are not confined to Europe. For thousands of years, people around the world have believed in similar creatures.

Kali

In India, followers of the Hindu religion consider a vampire-like creature named Kali to be a goddess. Kali can be destructive. She is often shown with fangs or a long tongue that drips blood. She also wears a necklace made of human heads.

Kali

21

Chiang-shih

The *chiang-shih*, a Chinese vampire, had red eyes and white hair. Some people believed that chiang-shih were dead bodies that had been taken over by demons. Others thought the corpses turned into monsters when a cat jumped over their graves.

chiang-shih

Asasabonsam

In Africa, people believed the *asasabonsam* hung from trees. Instead of feet, this vampire had hooks dangling from its legs. People passing underneath the trees got caught in the hooks. After feeding on blood, this monster chewed its victims with iron teeth.

Yara-ma-yha-who

The native people of Australia told stories of the *yara-ma-yha-who*. This little red man had suction cups on its fingers and toes. It lived in the tops of fig trees and waited for people to rest beneath them. This vampire then jumped on its victims and sucked their blood.

FACT:
Legend has it that anyone who was attacked by the yara-ma-yha-who more than once would turn into this monster.

yara-ma-yha-who

Asema

In South America, some old people were thought to be vampires called *asema*. They looked like normal people during the day. But at night they shed their skin and turned into balls of light. They then floated from place to place, sucking the blood of sleeping humans.

Penanggalan

In Malaysia, people feared the *penanggalan* vampire. They believed this female bloodsucker didn't have a body. Instead, bloody guts hung from a floating head. This vampire was thought to attack children.

penanggalan

chupacabra

FACT:

The Mexican *chupacabra* is a small gray creature with eyes that glow in the dark. It is thought to suck animal blood. Today people still debate whether or not this creature exists.

Chapter 5

POP CULTURE VAMPIRES

Vampires aren't real, yet they seem to be everywhere we look. Books, movies, and even breakfast cereals all feature vampires. Where did the idea of today's vampire come from?

Dracula's Inspiration

The pop culture vampire trend seemed to start with Bram Stoker's 1897 novel *Dracula*. In 1922, a new spin on the Dracula story hit movie theaters. The film *Nosferatu* featured a disgusting, undead vampire. This nasty character was very similar to the vampires of European folklore. But in 1931, the movie *Dracula* came out. Attractive actor Bela Lugosi played the smooth, gentleman-like Count Dracula. Ever since, the idea of the good-looking, yet deadly, vampire has fascinated audiences.

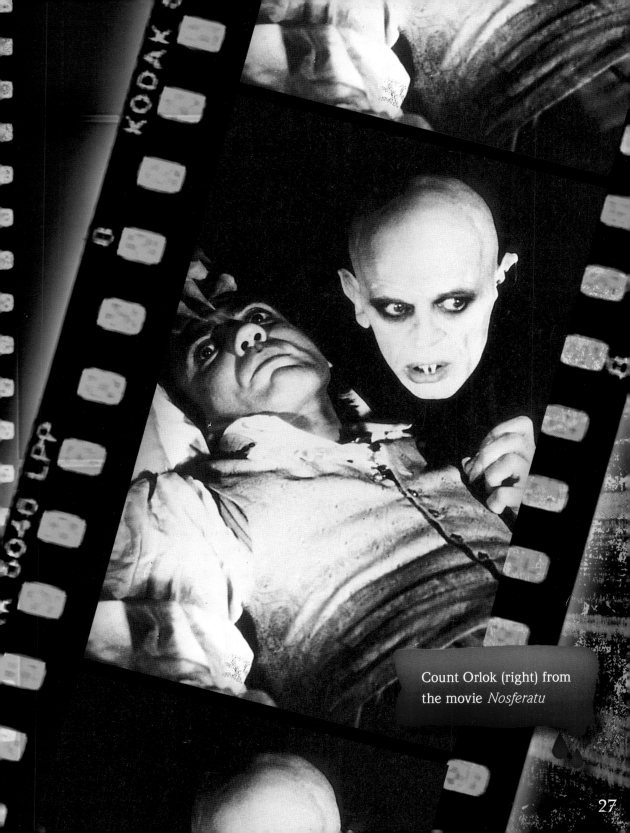

Count Orlok (right) from
the movie *Nosferatu*

Today's Vampires

Today the most popular vampire is the vampire with a soul. This vampire is often the hero in the story and fights "bad" vampires. He still has a thirst for blood. But he also has good looks and super strength. Most importantly, he has a heart.

The belief in real vampires is long gone. But thanks to books, TV shows, and movies, vampires are more popular today than ever. Perhaps it is the vampire's ability to live forever that appeals to people so much. Certainly the legends of vampires will live on for a very long time.

FACT:

The character of Edward Cullen in the *Twilight* books and movies is a "good" vampire. Instead of sucking the blood of humans, he satisfies his thirst with animal blood.

Actor Robert Pattinson played Edward Cullen in the *Twilight* movies.

The Real Dracula

Bram Stoker found the name "Dracula" in a history book while writing his vampire novel. He used the name for his evil main character. But the real Dracula was not a vampire at all. Vlad Dracula was a European prince. In the mid-1400s, Dracula ruled over the kingdom of Wallachia in modern-day Romania. He reigned during a time of intense fighting and wars.

Dracula was a cruel leader. Thousands of people died at his hands. When Dracula conquered a city, he burned it to the ground. Dracula impaled any survivors. Innocent people were not safe from Dracula's cruelty either. One story tells of Dracula inviting a large number of poor people to a banquet. When they finished eating, Dracula locked them inside a building and set it on fire.

Vlad Dracula

GLOSSARY

bloat (BLOHT)—a condition in which a dead body fills with gas or liquid as the tissues break down

contagious (kuhn-TAY-juhss)—easily spread; a contagious disease is spread by direct contact with someone or something already infected with it

corpse (KORPS)—a dead body

culture (KUHL-chuhr)—a people's way of life, ideas, customs, and traditions

eclipse (i-KLIPS)—an astronomical event in which Earth's shadow passes over the moon or the moon's shadow passes over Earth

hallucination (huh-loo-suh-NAY-shuhn)—something seen that is not really there

impale (im-PALE)—to thrust a sharpened stake through a person's body

microorganism (mye-kroh-OR-guh-niz-uhm)—a living thing too small to be seen without a microscope

plague (PLAYG)—a serious disease that spreads quickly to many people and often causes death

tuberculosis (tu-bur-kyuh-LOH-siss)—a disease caused by bacteria that causes fever, weight loss, and coughing; left untreated, tuberculosis can lead to death

READ MORE

Goldberg, Enid A., and Norman Itzkowitz.
Vlad the Impaler: The Real Count Dracula. A
Wicked History. New York: Franklin Watts, 2008.

Kallen, Stuart A. *Vampires.* The Mysterious and
Unknown. San Diego: ReferencePoint Press, 2008.

Oxlade, Chris. *The Mystery of Vampires and
Werewolves.* Can Science Solve? Chicago:
Heinemann Library, 2008.

Rainey, Rich. *Vampire Life.* Vampires. Mankato,
Minn.: Capstone Press, 2011.

INTERNET SITES

FactHound offers a safe, fun way to find Internet
sites related to this book. All of the sites on
FactHound have been researched by our staff.

Here's all you do:

Visit *www.facthound.com*

FactHound will fetch the best sites for you!

INDEX